THE
STARTING IN MA~~NAGEMENT~~
POCKETBOOK

By Patrick Forsyth
Drawings by Phil Hailstone

369 0123786

"An excellent introduction for the new manager. Even as an experienced manager I gained useful insights and reminders from this book."
Pippa Bourne, Head of Marketing and Business Development, Centre for Management Development

"A wardrobe-sized subject brilliantly condensed into a pocket-sized book. Straightforward, sound advice - much of it simple common sense once you are made aware of it. There's no need to attend expensive training courses; this book covers the subject perfectly."
Peter O'Riley, Learning & Development Manager, Ernst & Young

CONTENTS

INTRODUCTION
The Management Challenge

MORE WISE WORDS

Always take a job that is too big for you
Harry Emerson Fosdick

Are you worrying that you've done just that? Great! Anything less and you would not be aiming sufficiently high. Rising to the challenge is rewarding, as this pocketbook underlines.

INTRODUCTION

AN IMPORTANT STEP

So, now you're a manager. While it sounds good it also makes you think, or it should do. Becoming a manager may be a step up, but it is also wholly different from being in an executive role.

Management:

- Involves responsibility for others
- Is potentially very rewarding
- Is likely to be a challenge

The role demands specific approaches and skills, some of which you may not have used before. You need to adjust, and this pocketbook will help you do so - promptly, easily and with certainty. It provides guidelines to help you fit into your new role effectively and speedily, and achieve the results that you want.

First rule: don't underestimate the change involved in your transition to management.

PAUSE FOR THOUGHT

Generally, progress within an organisation (including the rewards that can accompany it) is inherently linked to a management role. Thus:

- Success at one thing leads to promotion into a *different* role
- Some of the skills that made you successful in the past may not help you as a manager
- Additional skills demanded by management may not play to your strengths
- The job of managing people may be something you enjoy for its own sake rather than something you're prepared to do because it takes you further up the hierarchy

Pause, reflect and consider: do you *really want to be a manager*? If not, consider other ways ahead. If you do, read on.

HOW TO APPROACH YOUR NEW ROLE

The extent to which you succeed in your new role will be influenced radically by the attitude you take to it. You should:

- See it as something new, involving different approaches from those used in the past (though don't throw the baby out with the bath water: your prior experience will be necessary)

- Aim to learn surely and fast, keep an open mind, beware of making unwarranted assumptions and consciously define and adopt new approaches

The remainder of this book focuses on:

- Those actions you should take in the first days and weeks in office, and the attitude you should adopt, which make a difference to your ultimate effectiveness

- Those aspects of the management process that you need to get to grips with in the early days and which have a disproportionate effect on success

MANAGEMENT DEFINED

Being a manager involves people - other people. You may still have your own work to do but, additionally, you have other people's work to consider.
At its simplest, management is:

● Achieving results *through* other people, with the aim of...

● Meeting specific, tangible, often financial, objectives

Management is *not* just about allocating work (deciding who does what); nor is it just about doing things *for* other people. The process of management takes time, effort and expertise.

Others must think you have management potential, so you have to prove them right.

(7)

INTRODUCTION

THE KEY TASKS

Once you have people reporting to you, the classic tasks involved in managing them are:

- Planning (what must be done to achieve the desired results)
- Organising (time, people and activities)
- Recruitment and selection (to create or replenish the team)
- Training and development (to keep people's skills sharp)
- Motivation (creating and maintaining positive attitudes amongst the team)
- Control (monitoring performance standards and taking action in the light of results)

And the overall orchestration of everything that all this, and whatever work the team does, implies.

You are going to need to keep a clear head, an eye on both the detail and the broad picture, and become expert at the skills the role demands.

THE KEY SKILLS

The task of management demands proficiency in a number of skills. These will vary depending on the exact nature of the job but are likely to include:

- Decision-making and problem-solving
- Time management
- Communications (business writing, making formal presentations, running meetings, one-to-one liaison with staff, interviewing, etc)

Your ability to manage people effectively can easily be hampered by shortfalls in your skill levels. Ensuring you have the skills for the job is, therefore, a key starting point.

Strength in your personal skills directly affects your potential ability to manage a group of people.

SKILLS CHECKLIST

At an early stage, list those skills that your new job demands. Next, rate your level of ability for each skill. Then, if appropriate, indicate the action you propose taking to improve the rating.

Skill	Rating	Action

Completing this exercise may stretch well beyond your appointment. Don't delay starting it.

SEEING THE FUTURE

The manager's responsibility includes creating a vision. This may sound intangible but it is not. It links closely with having clear objectives, yet goes further. The manager needs to create:

- Clarity of purpose
- A belief that delivering excellence is necessary, worthwhile and possible
- A feeling of interest (better still excitement) about achieving goals
- A link between the overall picture and the needs and satisfactions of the individual members of the team

Carefully think through this aspect of your new role, and make sure you have the information necessary to define a vision and know how you will put it over to others.

Where there is no vision the people perish
(Proverbs 29:18)

MANAGEMENT STYLE

What sort of manager are you going to be? What kind of manager *should* you aim to be? There are various ways to define styles of management. Five classic styles are:

- **Dictatorship**　　　　　　The manager decides on his or her own
- **Benevolent autocracy**　　The manager decides, the group advises
- **Democracy**　　　　　　　The group decides, the manager advises
- **Laissez-faire**　　　　　　Nobody makes proper decisions
- **Consultative**　　　　　　Manager asks, group contributes, manager decides

All styles have their place depending on the situation. Indeed, the situation must always be considered. In many instances what is needed is a blend of more than one style.

Overall, your style makes a difference. Nowadays that style should be characterised by *working with people* (the days of just telling staff what to do are long gone). You will have decisions to make about this.

Ultimately your style must play to your strengths, be acceptable to your staff – and aid effectiveness.

INTRODUCTION

FOCUS ON PRIORITIES

Pareto's Law (the 80/20 rule) states that 80% of results flows from just 20% of causes. Put another, personal, way: 20% of what you do contributes disproportionately to what you achieve.

This should give everyone pause for thought, especially managers. The consequences of their actions have a knock-on effect throughout their teams. In the worst case scenario, it can mean that the whole team is not concentrating on those things that have the greatest impact on results.

So, early on you must:

- Define and focus on your own priorities
- Make managing your people an unbreakable priority
- Work with them to ensure they work in a way that focuses on their core 20% of key tasks

The ultimate objective is to make the productivity of the whole team effective, and ensure everyone works in a way that reflects the realities of the 80/20 rule.

A GOOD BEGINNING

As a manager, your future success now depends not just on you but on your people. What view of you will they take? If they must have a manager then, doubtless, they will prefer a good one.

What will they find? They will be watching and waiting, and it will not take them long to form, at least, an initial view about you. First impressions last. People will:

- Observe you, your manner and style
- Listen to what you say and read between the lines
- Watch what you do and how you do it
- Consider how your actions affect them

For your part you must:

- Prepare thoroughly before you start
- Start as you mean to go on

You will not jump successfully into management by hoping to *make it up as you go along*. If you want a good start, you have to make it happen.

A GOOD BEGINNING

Everything that follows is predicated on the belief that you *can* make a success of management. It shows *how* you need to act and *what* action is necessary to become, and remain, a good manager.

Always bear in mind that success can only be gained through your actions. Never rely on good luck, though by all means take advantage of any that may come along.

Remember the saying, *luck is a matter of preparation meeting opportunity*. Let us turn now to what you can do to get ready ahead of the transition.

Note If you have already taken up a management post you may need to take action smartly regarding certain points covered in the next section.

NOTES

BEFORE TAKING UP YOUR <u>APPOINTMENT</u>

THE POWER OF PREPARATION

Be prepared really is a good motto. Once you are in the hot seat there may not be time for much reflection. Therefore, time and thought spent in advance are likely to prove invaluable.

Preparation can:

● Secure information, allowing appropriate decisions to be made

● Allow you to create a plan of action

● Ensure you are in a position to start as you mean to go on

● Give you confidence to proceed as you deem appropriate

In this way you will, at the very least, make it clear to people that you are prepared, and this will positively affect the profile you acquire. Systematic preparation is thus the order of the day.

Good managers do their homework, and this begins before the job starts.

SOME SERIOUS SELF-ANALYSIS

The next step is to analyse your strengths and weaknesses. It may help to think back to past appraisals. Be honest. Make a list. What are you good at and what are you not so good at? How well equipped are you for the work environment? Review:

- Skills
- Personality factors
- Knowledge (of the job, function, organisation, people, product – whatever is relevant)
- Connections (who you know may be as useful as what you know)
- Profile (how you are seen around the organisation)
- Attitudes (and how they affect your work and dealings with others)

BEFORE TAKING UP YOUR APPOINTMENT

THE MATCH BETWEEN YOU & THE JOB

Now look at yourself alongside the job description for your new position (this might even be something you can do, in part, in discussion with your own manager). See how you match up.

Ask questions such as:

- What skills need strengthening?
- Which aspects of my personality can I put to good use (or should I curb)?
- What areas of knowledge must I extend and how can I achieve this?
- Whom do I know who might be useful and with whom must I forge new links?

Be specific. Consider both the short- and long-term. Prioritise. For example: you conclude that you will be able to manage with your current level of report writing skills but how long will you survive if you do not know how to run – and maintain control of – a meeting? (Note: if this hits near to home get a copy of *The Meetings Pocketbook* at once!).

PLAN ACTION TO CREATE A MATCH

Analysis is no good unless it leads to action. Consider next what your analysis necessitates. In part it may demand you make a number of personal resolutions (I must curb my temper) but some elements will call for an action plan.

Remember how busy you will be when the job gets underway. List concrete proposals and get things moving where possible (again, this may need consultation with, or sanction from, your manager). For example, you may propose to:

- Arrange a meeting
- Attend a training course
- Locate specific information
- Gain certain experience

Remember, an action plan should specify what, who and when.

ACTION PLAN: EXAMPLE

Say, for instance, you resolve to improve your report writing skills because your new role involves regular work of this nature. Your action plan could look something like this:

- Read up about it
- Attend a training course
- Ask someone to critique a couple of my reports – perhaps both before and after the course
- Obtain from my new manager a clear specification regarding the length, style, presentation, etc, of reports

Keep this plan in mind when you take up your new post and relate it to your timetable and diary.

RECONNAISSANCE MODE

Forewarned is forearmed goes the old saying. Never is this more apt than when you are stepping into uncharted territory.

Ahead of starting your management job, you need to ask yourself what up-to-date information it might be useful (or essential) to have in advance. You might check things like:

- Targets (Is my new group and each member of it on target, lagging behind or ahead? Why is this?)

- Procedures and systems (What should I familiarise myself with ahead of my involvement?)

- People (Do I know the new team? How well? Should I meet any of them, either individually or collectively, *before* I take up my appointment? Can I organise an introduction through someone who knows them, such as their existing manager?)

Continued

RECONNAISSANCE MODE

Checklist continued from previous page:

- Lines of communication and reporting (Who do I and my team have contact with and in what way? What processes, such as meetings and reports, are involved?)

- Controls (How will I monitor performance and progress?)

- Policy (Do I know what applies in my new situation and do I understand my role?)

- Records (What should I look at? Consider everything from notes about people's last job appraisal to the contents of the stationery cupboard.)

Be thorough here; information really is power.

BEFORE TAKING UP YOUR APPOINTMENT

PERMANENT PROCESSES

In addition to the one-off actions referred to earlier, you should consider those actions that you can take in advance which will have ongoing implications for yourself and your team. In other words, get ready those things that…

- You will definitely want to do (you may be sure that a particular reporting format is necessary and appropriate, for example) and those things that…

- You feel likely to be appropriate (you may want to spend less time here but still want to be in a position to act promptly if your feeling proves right).

As part of your preparation, think through how you will explain, justify and announce your plans.

Take care not to let your enthusiasm run away with you, as there is more you still have to learn about the situation you will shortly step into.

ANNOUNCING THE NEWS

A wrong basis for the announcement
may take a long time from which
to recover.

Moral: *this is something to anticipate and influence.*

ANNOUNCING THE NEWS

What will people hear about your appointment? It is worth checking how the change in your responsibilities will be announced, especially if you work for an organisation of any size.

- Ask how your new staff will be told, and ask too if you can see in advance any note that will be sent to them. If necessary, try and influence what is said. The announcement should position what is happening as a positive move, explaining as required.

- Ditto wider notification: check who else will be told and how. Will the announcement appear on notice-boards (electronic or otherwise)? Should it feature in any corporate newsletter? And so on.

At the very least, you should know what has been said to people before you walk through the door on day one. More likely you will want to influence what is said, how it is put and who receives the message.

BEFORE YOU TAKE UP YOUR APPOINTMENT

THINKING ABOUT DAY ONE

Beyond the general and broad preparation referred to, you need to think – specifically – about your first day (or two) in situ. You don't want to get caught up doing nothing but responding to events, and you don't want to appear unapproachable just because the priority seems to be reading files.

So, as far as is possible decide:

- **What you will do.** For example, convene a staff meeting (With what agenda?), get up to date on the current situation, organise your own workload, check your diary, etc.

- **What you will arrange/announce.** For example, setting and announcing dates and times for various discussions, meetings and decisions, asking people for their views (to be put forward in writing or discussed later at a meeting), etc.

- **What you will not do** (or not immediately, for whatever reason).

Resolve NOT to be railroaded into making instant decisions in response to urgent requests (or demands). However, make it clear that you will consider such requests promptly (and do not forget).

STARTING
AS YOU MEAN TO GO ON

STARTING AS YOU MEAN TO GO ON

BEGIN WITH YOUR PEOPLE IN MIND

Before you do anything, have the likely expectations of your people in mind. They will tend to define a good manager as one who:

- Is positive and enthusiastic
- Has vision (sees the longer/broader view)
- Achieves their own goals
- Is well organised
- Makes good – objective – decisions
- Delegates appropriately
- Provides good – honest – feedback
- Is fair and has no favourites
- Is open-minded and curious

- Listens (and is available to listen)
- Knows and takes an interest in staff
- Encourages/supports staff development
- Communicates well
- Shows confidence and gives credit
- Keeps people informed
- Acknowledges own mistakes/weaknesses
- Shares experience

BEGIN WITH YOUR PEOPLE IN MIND

Similarly, people will have firm views on the type of manager they do *not* want.
Those, for example, who:

- Put themselves before their people
- Fail to set clear objectives/priorities
- Don't appear to care about the team (a loner)
- Are secretive (or late in informing)
- Procrastinate
- Are unapproachable

- Are not honest, open and fair
- Fail to consider people's feelings
- Let their personal workload prevent team maintenance

This list and the preceding one could easily be extended and will
be influenced by factors that are especially important in your job,
organisation or function.

**Make it your business to discover what is most
important to your people.**

NEW POST – NEW EMPLOYER?

Throughout your planning and progress you need to tailor your approach depending on whether you are moving positions within your current company or moving to a new one.

- **Existing employer.** Keep in mind that people know you. Your position relative to others will – must – change. You have to create a suitable *distance* between you and others, and not allow existing relationships (and friendships) to dictate the way things work. At the same time you are (still) part of the team, and how this manifests itself needs consideration. Beware being arrogant. Do not throw the baby out with the bath water – old alliances can help.

- **New employer.** The learning curve you face is inevitably much steeper. Beware of acting (or even of giving a view) before you have sufficient facts.

Always match your approach to the actual circumstances and be realistic about the situation you are in.

STARTING AS YOU MEAN TO GO ON

FIRST THINGS FIRST

Day one as a manager: a great deal to consider if you are moving into a new situation. You should:

- **See your new manager early on:** confirm your role and priorities and set up communications procedure between you both, especially to make clear how you check things during the first few days.

- **Arrange introductions to other key people:** if your work involves contacts with others (another department, people on the same level as you, etc), make sure you know them and begin to cultivate a relationship from the word go.

- **Meet your own staff:** (more of this anon).

Once again, remember that *you only get one chance to make a good first impression* – especially in a new environment. This may be a cliché, but it's true. So, consider the details and get them right. For example:

- Be sure to arrive on time (or a touch early)
- Look the part (think about what you wear)

STARTING AS YOU MEAN TO GO ON

MEET THE PEOPLE

Make a point of speaking to everyone on day one. If this is not possible (for example, someone may be away) set a time for an initial word. This can be informal (just a word at their desk) or in your office or meeting room. It needs to do various things:

- Act as a personal introduction
- Clarify, briefly, how you see their role (or how the other person sees it)
- Dispel any immediate fears the team member may have
- Answer any immediate questions (or say when they can and will be answered)
- Begin to show you as the kind of manager you want to be
- Ask questions and canvass opinion from the team (about how things are going, what might need change, challenges for the future, etc)

Keep these exchanges positive. Do not be afraid to put things on ice for the moment but be specific - *I can't answer that now; give me a day or two and I will say something about that when the whole team gets together.*

Keep notes – and keep promises made during such conversations.

ASSESS THE PEOPLE

You need to begin to get the measure of people early on. Beware of thinking you are an expert psychologist, but do:

- Listen to what people say and how they say it
- Read between the lines
- Check immediately anything that is unclear
- Address (or note) any apparent hidden agendas
- Be aware of the informal communications channels as well as the hierarchical ones
- Note any areas requiring further investigation

You need to get to know people, their working methods, strengths and weaknesses. This cannot be done in five minutes; start early and handle it objectively.

Beware of making and acting on unwarranted, instant assumptions about people.

STARTING AS YOU MEAN TO GO ON

A FIRST STAFF MEETING

Get the team together as soon as possible, on the first day if you can. Remember, your meetings speak volumes about the kind of manager you are. Plan to make them really effective, therefore.

- Set the time and date to be as convenient to people as possible (you may need to check this with a new group)
- Organise the administration (place, refreshments, acting to stop interruptions, etc)
- Issue a clear agenda in advance
- Make sure the agenda is worthwhile, fits the time available and is useful for those attending
- Tell people what you expect from them (for instance, if someone is to give you a run down on their section or work, let them plan how to do it from your clear brief)

Continued

A FIRST STAFF MEETING

- Set start and finish times – and try to stick to them (you are setting up habits here so be sure to start *on time*)

- Give people a say – listen – make notes and be seen to take an interest in their views

- Make any action points clear (whether for the group or for individuals)

- Link to the next meeting (you might set a date)

- Confirm anything necessary in writing

A meeting should motivate. People will wonder how your presence and style will affect them. Show them your impact will be beneficial. Spell out how.

STARTING AS YOU MEAN TO GO ON

A FIRST STAFF MEETING

The agenda for this first meeting will depend on your precise role. It is likely to include items such as:

- Your understanding of the team's role and immediate goals
- Any necessary explanations for change (eg: why you are now manager)
- The current position (progress, problems, opportunities)
- A chance to ask questions
- Details of, and reasons for, any immediate changes
- Reporting and communications procedures (eg: when and how you plan to keep in touch with individuals and the group)
- Action points on immediate operational issues

You should ask as much as inform, and not change existing procedures without good reasons (and knowing the facts). However logical changes may be, people will be suspicious *(Will it adversely affect me?)* so see, and explain things, from their point of view.

Empathy is your greatest ally in the early stages of managing a group.

STARTING AS YOU MEAN TO GO ON

EARLY ISSUE: EARLY ACTION

Here is something to do as soon as possible (though always with a firm basis of information). Identify an issue waiting for attention and which is *seen as needing attention*. And sort it out.

Something where you can:

- Tell people you recognise it is a priority, one that must not be left
- Explain the basis of a decision
- Specify action to be taken (this could be a temporary measure)
- Take any additional action necessary (eg: confirm in writing, consult or advise further afield than your section)
- Get it off the department's *to do* list promptly and definitely

You need a task that is seen as due (overdue?) for action, one that will also be seen as well resolved – an example of how you mean to go on. **Select carefully, act in a considered fashion and this will not only clear an outstanding issue but will also say something positive about you.**

GROUND RULES

Consultation is important to the management process but there are times when arguments must be avoided and an authoritative approach taken. If every initiative involved lengthy consultation, time would run out, little would get done and we would all be in trouble.

You might, for example, consult about departmental policy on dress code or what can be claimed on expenses. Then – for a while at least – what is decided (what you decide) assumes the status of a rule. It is expected that people toe the line, and no time is wasted on endless arguments about *exceptions*. In due course you may need to reassess the situation and possibly change the rules.

The same can be said of meetings *(When we set the date for a staff meeting, we all stick to it and start on time)* and procedures *(When certain documents are sent out you get a copy – always).*

How you act in this kind of way affects your profile as a manager. If people say of you: *If you attend one of Patrick's meetings you'd better be on time,* it is surely a good thing – as long as they believe you are a manager who understands their point of view as well.

STARTING AS YOU MEAN TO GO ON

LAYING DOWN THE LAW

Sometimes a manager has to face awkward, contentious, embarrassing or tough issues. Difficult situations, you may have noticed, don't tend to get easier if delayed or ignored. For the manager, dealing with such problems goes with the territory.

It is one of the things people watch for. They wonder: *How will this person react under pressure? What happens when we stand up to this person or make something awkward?* The answer is simple – show them.

It may be better if you pick your ground early on, by finding a situation that will demonstrate that you have the clout to succeed in management. Thus:

- Select a suitable circumstance (something you're sure of and which matters)
- Make a stand, be adamant – explain, by all means, but stick to your guns
- Don't back down (pressure to do so at this stage may be in the nature of a test)
- Let the word go round – *this person's no soft touch*

STARTING AS YOU MEAN TO GO ON

FORGING ALLIANCES

All sorts of people, regardless of level and position, can be of help to you – now and ongoing. They may be:

- A source of information and advice
- A link to other people
- A provider of moral support
- Part of the new mix of social contacts you will need in your new role

Make a list, initiate contact as necessary and maintain contact at an appropriate level of frequency and in whatever way suits (eg: formal meetings, cups of coffee and e-mails).

Those people who may be of help include your immediate line manager, their manager, mentors, staff and assorted contacts and 'buddies', as well as those in specifically useful functional roles (eg: training).

Ensure that the relationships you develop are two-way: you must give as well as take if they are to succeed. Strike a proper balance.

MATTERS OF DISCIPLINE

Discipline is unlikely to come up for a while. However, it is certainly important enough to deserve comment in case the matter does arise.

Never duck or delay matters of staff discipline.

- Check the situation *very carefully*
- If facts are not clear check them out but do not delay long and set a specific time for further action
- Deal with the matter of itself (don't feel you have to be lenient because it's day one)
- Take action and check it against policy (If a warning is necessary, for example, should it be in writing, how expressed, where filed and who should be copied?)
- Remember the key task is to secure the future
- Be fair and do not go over the top to register your power

Appropriate action is likely to be approved by the team. Being seen as a soft touch can create problems for the future.

STARTING AS YOU MEAN TO GO ON

HOW YOU WILL WORK WITH PEOPLE

There could well be matters you're sure of and want to instigate early on. For example, you may want regular meetings, certain things put in writing, files organised in a particular way, and so on. Certainly, you may wish to make clear aspects of the management process itself: reporting procedures, checks and controls, regular and informal communications – how you will work with people one to one and as a group. All needs to be clear.

If so, and especially if processes change, then:

- Communicate formally (normally in writing)
- Explain what you're doing and why
- Position it as a trial, if necessary (Why not? You can build in any good feedback and may possibly be grateful for an opportunity to make further changes, without it looking as if you don't know what you're doing)

Provide feedback and thank people for fitting in and taking the extra time. Show them how the changes will help you – and them.

STARTING AS YOU MEAN TO GO ON

POSITIONING YOURSELF AS MANAGER

Ask yourself what characteristics will make you the sort of manager you want to be. *What would your staff say?*

Make a list. For example: being knowledgeable, confident, well organised, looking the part, efficient, decisive…whatever.

The list should point to the type of manager you *intend* to be and the characteristics you *intend* to project. It is not a list of what you are or are not. If there are any aspects you feel you should work at or emphasise, make a note of these.

By all means, tell people how you intend to operate but remember that they are more likely to form an opinion about you based on what you do rather than *what you say*.

STARTING AS YOU MEAN TO GO ON

SOCIALISING WITH COLLEAGUES

Fact: offices are social environments. This will not change and there is no reason why you should be excluded just because you are now 'in charge'. But you do need to approach social gatherings, whether momentary (a cup of coffee and a chat) or more formal (someone's leaving 'do'), with some deference.

It may help to categorise such contacts as follows:

1. **Those that are part of the formal hierarchy**. It is perfectly possible to have a comfortable and informal social chat across hierarchical boundaries. These encounters are, as it were, 'asides' to the normal work relationship.

2. **Those where everyone is 'off duty'**. In such cases work relationships are put more firmly to one side and everyone is regarded as equal.

Understand that there needs to be a line – recognised by all – beyond which you should don your manager's hat. Every group needs to evolve its own culture about such matters. A little drunken tomfoolery at an office party might, for example, be tolerated (and quickly forgotten) but someone insulting or assaulting the M.D. should warrant your intervention. And if it is you who is drunk – beware!

THE ROLE OF COMMUNICATIONS

Nothing puts you in the *bad manager* category more swiftly than poor communications skills. Staff see an inadequate communicator as someone who is unclear, ambiguous, says too little, speaks up too late or not at all (keeps secrets unnecessarily) and, most importantly, someone who doesn't relate to their viewpoint.

Resolve to communicate:

- Using appropriate methods (memo or meeting, e-mail or notice-board)

- From the right perspective (talk about *we* not *I* and put things personally – *You will find* rather than *This is the case*)

- Using good communications principles (keep it simple, make it clear, be precise and succinct … and more)

- Explaining both the what *and* the why of things

Communications is one of the most important aspects of your job. If you feel you need to bone up on it, do so. Ignoring failings or uncertainties risks disaster.

Your early communications will be looked at or listened to carefully. Lines will be read between and inferences about you, and the way you do things, will be drawn – for good or ill. Take care.

THE ROLE OF COMMUNICATIONS

While thinking about communications, make one firm rule for yourself:

Always be courteous to your staff.

The old adage that politeness costs nothing is true. Any temptation that staff may provide to descend into insults or, even, to be offhand may cause problems and will certainly not engender respect. This applies whatever the provocation – and, believe me, sooner or later if you manage people there will be some!

So, keep cool, count to ten if necessary and moderate your language and your manner.

THE ROLE OF COMMUNICATIONS

A final point about communications is that you need to be constantly well informed about what is going on: in your department, around the organisation and in any other area that is important to you.

Never forget that *informal* communications are as important here as formal ones.

The need for a good network of contacts has already been mentioned. Here we flag the importance of **the grapevine**. This exists in *every* organisation.

- Discover how it works and who is key to its operation
- Get yourself *plugged in*
- Remember that communication is two-way (you must contribute to receive)
- Use it constructively: ignore and do not start rumours, use it for firm information, early warning and dissemination, and **keep your eyes and ears open**

NOTES

CREATING STAFF LOYALTY & COMMITMENT

TAKING SIDES

As a manager you have a juggling act to perform, one which balances different points of view, classically those of:

- Yourself
- The organisation
- Your department (or division, section)
- Your people
- External contacts (eg: customers or suppliers)

Sometimes (regularly?) conflicts arise: something is right for the department and the people, but not for either the organisation or you. On occasions you will find yourself disagreeing with a company policy but having to support it even though you know that your people see it as wrong and personally inconvenient.

How you handle this balancing act is important, and it may be necessary to explain the reasons behind your actions. It is an area for some consistency.

CREATING STAFF LOYALTY & COMMITMENT

TAKING SIDES

You need to keep certain factors in mind when balancing the interests of different parties:

- First and foremost your responsibility is to the organisation and to achieving the targets set for you

- You can only do this with the support of your people, so in the long-term you must carry them with you (some disagreement may be seen as inevitable)

- You have a responsibility upwards and downwards within the organisation (perhaps one answer is to support a policy, insisting that your people comply, while communicating upwards in an attempt to have it changed if it can be bettered)

- You must never be seen as selfish, simply acting to make your own lot better (this will, rightly, always be resented)

- You must sometimes be *seen* to fight your corner on behalf of your section and its people (this will be appreciated, more so if what you take issue with is a nonsense and, especially, if you win!)

Early on as a manager, seek to demonstrate your skills at balancing different interests.

CREATING STAFF LOYALTY & COMMITMENT

TAKING SIDES

As well as making clear your position in respect of the organisation and the other *players,* you need to consider – and make clear – the relationship between you and your own staff.

You must always be fair (but rarely democratic). People must see the realities involved. They must understand that there is a balance and that you cannot always be automatically *on their side,* right or wrong.

Make it clear that you:

- See your success as tied in with and, indeed, dependent on them

- See your role as essentially supportive (in all sorts of ways: guidance, counselling, development and motivation)

- Believe that by working together you can all succeed – not just by everyone doing their share of the work but by *everyone* contributing creatively (ideas may come from anywhere)

> *I don't know the key to success, but the key to failure is trying to please everybody*
> Bill Crosby

DEALING WITH POOR PERFORMANCE

Poor performance is an issue that faces any manager from time to time. You can deal with it in several ways:

- Put up with it (not to be recommended)
- Re-brief or train to allow performance to improve
- Re-assign the person to another task that they can do
- Terminate employment

These options are linked. For example, you should only fire an under-performer having first explored the options of training or re-assignment. If having taken up these options there is no improvement, then more drastic action may be necessary and justified.

Do not put off taking action because you worry about the reaction of others. Provided action is justified it will almost certainly be approved.

Most team members hate passengers and are conscious that they and their colleagues have to make up the difference.

CREATING STAFF LOYALTY & COMMITMENT

A MAJOR PRINCIPLE

There is one maxim that, while it may initially seem somewhat obtuse, should be a guiding principle for every manager – and one to take on board early on. It is simply stated: **as a manager you cannot have the power and the credit.**

This means that you have to think in terms of the team. If you want to get things done – and have the power to make things happen – then you have to give other people the credit for what they do. Never:

- Pass off their ideas as yours (even when you contributed to their origination)

- Talk about *what I have done* when you mean what *we* or, better still, *they* or *you* have done

- Fail to give credit, within the group and beyond

You depend on your people. Do not seek credit for what they do; they will, rightly, resent it. And that will adversely affect their performance. If you want credit, it must come from what you do to make your people effective.

CREATING STAFF LOYALTY & COMMITMENT

WHO IS IN CHARGE?

The answer to this is clear – you are. The hierarchy means something and you should never apologise for it. Supervision works best when it is not overt but, ultimately, there must be supervision. This means:

- Making it clear when, where, how and on what issues your approval is required

- Keeping control of key issues, while thinking carefully about what they are and where you can empower people to make their own decisions

- Recognising that the buck stops with you, facing issues, making decisions and never saying you will deal with things and then sidelining or endlessly postponing them

- Being prepared to stick your neck out sometimes and always having the courage of your convictions

Your people must never doubt who is in charge. If you look like a doormat (even for a second) people will walk all over you. Credibility – once lost – is hard to win back.

CREATING STAFF LOYALTY & COMMITMENT

BEING PART OF THE TEAM

You are in authority. You must make decisions and ensure that rules and procedures are followed. But you will not win the hearts and minds of people by being aloof. You carry people with you best by:

- Leading from the front
- Getting involved
- Getting your hands dirty occasionally (regularly?)
- Knowing what is going on so that you are able to do all this

People will support those whom they feel understand – and, importantly, have experience of – their situation and are genuinely part of the team. They like it when you pitch in during an emergency (all hands to the pumps) but don't pick the easiest task! They like it when you sometimes take a turn making the tea or refuelling the photocopier.

Aim to become part of the team sooner rather than later.

MANAGING MEANS MOTIVATION

Resolve now – right now – that you will give motivation priority. Don't be mistaken, motivation makes a difference – a big difference. People perform better when they feel positive about their job. You must:

- Recognise that active motivation is necessary
- Resolve to spend regular time on it
- Not chase after magic formulae that will make it easy (there are none)
- Give attention to the detail
- Remember that you succeed by creating an impact that is cumulative in effect and tailored to your people

> *If you think you can, you can and if you think you can't, you're right*
> Mary Kay Ash

Your intention should be to make people feel, individually and as a group, that they are special. Doing so is the first step to making sure that what they do is special.

CREATING STAFF LOYALTY & COMMITMENT

UNDERSTANDING MOTIVATION

The detail here is important but beyond the scope of this book (see *The Motivation Pocketbook*). Every manager needs to know something of how motivation works. The key is to influence the *motivational climate* by taking action to:

- **Reduce negative influences.** Potentially, the good feelings people have about their jobs can be diluted by negative views on matters such as: company policy and administrative processes, supervision (that's you, unless you are careful!), working conditions, salary, relationships with peers (and others), impact on personal life, status and security. Action is necessary in all these areas to counteract any negative elements.

- **Increase positive influences.** Positive feelings can be strengthened by specific inputs in the areas of: achievement, recognition, the work itself, responsibility, advancement and growth.

Many factors contribute to the motivational climate - from ensuring that a system is as sensible and convenient to people as possible (reducing negative policy/working conditions), to just saying *well done* sufficiently often (recognising achievement).

UNDERSTANDING MOTIVATION

The state of motivation of a group or individual can be likened to a balance. There are pluses on one side and minuses on the other. All vary in size. The net effect of all the influences at a particular time decides the state of the balance and whether – overall – things are seen as positive, or not.

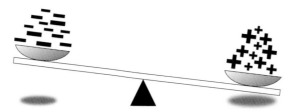

Changing the balance is thus a matter of detail with, for example, several small positive factors being able to outweigh what is seen as a major dis-satisfier.

CREATING STAFF LOYALTY & COMMITMENT

A LITTLE THOUGHT GOES A LONG WAY

You need to make it clear from the outset that you are concerned that people get job satisfaction. Major schemes can wait. Early on:

- **Take the *motivational temperature*:** investigate how people feel now (this is what you have to work on).

- **Consider the motivational implications of everything you do:** when implementing a new system, making a change, setting up a new regular meeting or whatever, consider what people will think about it? Will *they* see it as positive?

- **Use the small things – regularly:** for example, if asked if you have said *well done* often enough lately, you must always be able to answer *yes* – honestly.

- **Never be censorious:** you must not judge other people's motivation by your own feelings. Maybe they worry about things that strike you as silly or unnecessary. So be it. The job is to deal with it, not to rule it out as insignificant.

Create the habit of making motivation a key part of your management style and doing so will stand you in good stead. If you care about the people (really care) it will always show.

CREATING STAFF LOYALTY & COMMITMENT

KEEP IN TOUCH

Take away communications from an organisation and not much is left. Yet, the subject is often neglected. **It is the foundation of a good relationship between manager and staff, and thus the basis for success.**

Make sure you take action to create good – *two-way* – communications by, for example:

- **Practising MBWA:** that is *Management By Walking About*. Talk to people informally, ask, listen, take note and ensure feedback.

- **Regularly informing people of your thinking:** by memo, e-mail, at meetings, etc. Tell them what your vision is, what you plan, hope and intend, what's happening – *and how it will affect them.*

- **Systematise the processes involved:** make aspects of what you do formal and regular (eg: regular departmental meetings and updates on operational issues).

Fundamental to good management is being seen as open and honest, concerned that people should know what is going on and concerned also to encourage and receive their inputs.

THE POWER OF CONSISTENCY

People work successfully with managers of all sorts, the tough and the tender. However, nothing, but nothing, throws them more than a manager who runs hot and cold – sweetness and light one minute (and ready to listen and consult) and doom and gloom the next (just demanding that people *Do what I say*).

Early on you may need to experiment a little with how you handle matters. That apart, you should try to adopt a consistent style. For example, let people know that:

- You will always make time for them (soon, and at an agreed time, if not instantly).
- You never prevaricate. Decisions may not be made instantly – if they need thought or consultation – but nor will they be endlessly avoided. If there must be some delay, tell people why and when things will be settled.

Make sure people understand *how* you approach things and *what* your attitude is to problems, opportunities and so on. While solutions will undoubtedly vary, your method and style of working should be largely a known quantity. **People like to know where they are and work better when they do.**

WORKING WITH PEOPLE
TO ACHIEVE RESULTS

WORKING TOGETHER

The principle of working together with your team should underpin how you operate. Once again, it helps to make this clear early on.

Managing people doesn't just mean acting as overseer, to see that they get their work done satisfactorily. It means involving people throughout the team in a creative role, to ensure that together you are all able to succeed.

Involving people on broad issues is motivational. Never underestimate people. Their views can enhance everything: methods, standards, processes and overall effectiveness.

Remember, managers are not paid to have all the ideas that are necessary to keep their section working well in a changing world, but they *are* paid to make sure that there are *enough* ideas to make things work and go on working.

Use your people and make it clear to them that you want and value their contributions.

UNDERPINNING SUCCESS

Some matters are of particular importance to the way a manager and staff work together. This is not the place to review the whole management process, but the following four areas are key and must be addressed correctly early on if results are to follow.

They are:

1. Setting goals
2. Project management
3. Ongoing development
4. Job performance appraisal

A quick look at each of these in turn...

SETTING GOALS

If you don't know where you are going any road will do. For all its familiarity and common sense this maxim is worth reiterating. No one and no organisation works well without clear objectives. The responsibility for setting many of them may well now be yours.

Objectives will only be clear if they are **SMART**:

Specific   so that they are clearly understood and no misunderstanding is possible

Measurable   so that everyone knows whether they have hit them, or not

Achievable   because if they are simply pie in the sky they will be ignored and you, and any future process of objective setting, will lose credibility

Realistic   in the sense that they must logically fit within the broad picture and be a desirable way of proceeding

Timed   without clear timing they will become meaningless

The objectives you set must condition and direct what your people do. Make sure everyone has clear goals from day one onwards.

PROJECT MANAGEMENT

Many of the tasks to be done involve the complex process of people working together in a co-ordinated way over time. When this is headed up by you or involves you, make sure that the project is:

- Carefully and systematically planned and organised
- Effectively executed
- Precisely monitored
- Fine-tuned so that contingencies and changes are accommodated
- Brought in on time, on spec and, if appropriate, on budget

Your management of others will be jeopardised if the way you organise the work of the section in any way falters.

ONGOING DEVELOPMENT

Nothing is so important to people as their success. Time and again you hear people say something like *Above all, I want to work with a manager from whom I can learn*. The development of your people is not something to ignore or leave to training departments. The responsibility is yours.

Make sure people have the right knowledge, skills and attitudes to do the jobs you want and to do them well. Development is not only about correcting weaknesses, it is about upgrading and taking people forward, not least to keep up with change.

Tell people that you:

- Recognise that their development is important
- Will help them gain experience and extend skills

And:

- Create a visible system so to do

As the old saying goes, you can either *have five years' experience or one year's experience multiplied by five*. People want the former. Show them you are the means to achieve it.

ONGOING DEVELOPMENT

Use the development cycle:

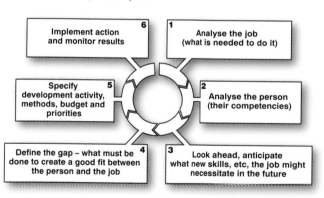

6 Implement action and monitor results

1 Analyse the job (what is needed to do it)

5 Specify development activity, methods, budget and priorities

2 Analyse the person (their competencies)

4 Define the gap – what must be done to create a good fit between the person and the job

3 Look ahead, anticipate what new skills, etc, the job might necessitate in the future

This is a rolling cycle. Keep clear records, make sure everyone is reviewed in this way and create a culture in which people value development and what it brings. **Part of your job is helping people to learn.**

SOME EARLY DEVELOPMENT

Development is sufficiently important to people (as well as being important in its own right) for you to address the process and give out the right messages about it early on.

You may, sensibly, not want to send everyone off on a course in your first five minutes, so consider other actions, asking:

- Should development be on the agenda for meetings?
- Can anything be done on-the-job? (In any case, a key part of the manager's personal responsibility for development.)
- Can any ongoing actions be instigated now? (A simple monthly lunchtime session, perhaps.)

The culture of an organisation in terms of its attitude to training and development is important to people. Their view of it is, in part, dependent on you. **Send the right signals.**

WORKING WITH PEOPLE TO ACHIEVE RESULTS

JOB PERFORMANCE APPRAISAL

In many organisations appraisals are poorly conducted and rated unhelpful by those who are appraised. **A good rule for new managers is to make the first staff appraisal you conduct a memorable experience.**

Appraisals should:

- Be constructive, helpful and motivational

- Focus on the future

- Be a genuine opportunity for both parties to ensure that the period ahead (year, quarter, etc) goes well, perhaps better than the last

- Link to action plans for the future

Study your organisation's appraisal system and learn how to conduct an effective appraisal meeting. This is good use of management time. Apart from helping you achieve results in a practical sense, it will also position you as a competent manager and differentiate you from others.

MANAGEMENT PROCESSES

The previous pages have dealt with a number of individual areas that are important to the management process and to the new manager. Whatever processes you are setting up, they will be seen as a sign of your style. If they meet with approval, trust is built. If not, they distance you from your staff.

Ensure systems and processes are:
- Fair
- Understandable
- Relevant
- Time (and cost) effective
- Effective

And are **not**:
- Bureaucratic
- Out of touch with realities
- Over complex
- Restrictive/contradictory
- Incompatible with other systems/common sense

Everything you set up (or maintain if someone else instigated it) must aid the effectiveness and efficiency of the section. Those who do the work will quickly see inappropriate systems as you making their jobs more difficult; not a way you want to be seen. As the advertising slogan of the Abbey National bank says, *Life's complicated enough.*

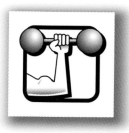

ADDING STRENGTH
TO THE TEAM

GETTING THE BEST FROM THE TEAM

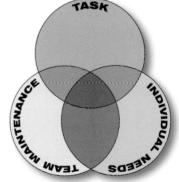

Recognise from the beginning that
your effectiveness depends on the team
and on the interaction of the three factors
shown in the diagram here:

You **must**:

- Ensure continuous
  task achievement

- Meet the needs
  of the group

- Meet the needs of
  individual group members

**This balance must always be kept in mind
(though some compromise may be necessary).**

GETTING THE BEST FROM THE TEAM

Your own best contribution to getting things done is ideally approached systematically. You must:

- Be clear exactly what the tasks are
- Understand how they relate to the objectives of the organisation (short- and long-term)
- Plan how they can be accomplished
- Define and provide the resources needed for accomplishment
- Create a structure and organisation of people that facilitates effective action
- Control progress as necessary during task completion
- Evaluate results, compare with objectives and fine-tune action and method for the future

The following three checklists relate back to the diagram on the facing page and highlight the thinking that is necessary here.

77

GETTING THE BEST FROM THE TEAM
CHECKLIST 1: ACHIEVING THE TASK

Ask yourself:

- Am I clear about my own responsibilities and authority?
- Am I clear about the department's agreed objectives?
- Have I a plan to achieve these objectives?
- Are jobs best structured to achieve what is required?
- Are working conditions/resources suited?
- Does everyone know their agreed targets/standards?
- Are the group competencies as they should be?
- Are we focused on priorities?
- Are those areas in which I'm personally involved well organised?
- Do I have the information necessary to monitor progress?
- Is management continuity assured in my absence?
- Am I seeing ahead and seeing the broad picture?
- Do I set a suitable example?

GETTING THE BEST FROM THE TEAM
CHECKLIST 2: MEETING THE INDIVIDUAL NEEDS

Ask yourself if each individual:

- Feels a sense of personal achievement from what they do and the contribution it makes
- Feels their job is challenging, demands the best of them and matches their capabilities
- Receives suitable recognition for what they do
- Has control of areas of work for which they are accountable
- Feels that they are advancing in terms of experience and ability

Many questions stem from this about what people do, how they do it, how what they do is organised and how they feel about it. It is worth thinking through what you need to ask regarding your own particular team.

GETTING THE BEST FROM THE TEAM

CHECKLIST 3: TEAM MAINTENANCE

To involve the whole team in pulling together towards individual and joint objectives, ask yourself, do I:

- Set team objectives clearly and make sure they are understood?
- Ensure standards are understood (and the consequences of not meeting them are understood and approved)?
- Find opportunities to create teamworking?
- Minimise any dissatisfaction?
- Seek and welcome new ideas?
- Consult appropriately and often enough?
- Keep people fully informed (about the long- and short-term)?
- Reflect the team's views in dealings with senior management?
- Accurately convey organisational policy to the team and reflect such policy in their objectives?

An analytical approach to these areas is the foundation to making your operation work effectively – and thus to getting tasks done effectively.

ADDING STRENGTH TO THE TEAM

A DYNAMIC ORGANISATION

The organisational structure of a team is important. Who does what, how one job relates to another, the lines of reporting and communication – all affect effectiveness. This is something to assess early on and watch on a regular basis. You should, therefore:

- Make sure that the structure you inherited fits the tasks to be done

- Implement any changes on a considered basis

- Explain changes positively (they may be seen with suspicion)

- Keep the organisation under review to ensure you retain a good *fit* between it and what it must do (external as well as internal changes or pressures can affect this)

- Fine-tune as necessary with an eye on tasks, individuals and the team as a whole

Any, even slight, incongruities about the way people are organised can easily dilute overall effectiveness. Do not change for change's sake, but do not expect things to remain as they are forever without needing change.

ADDING STRENGTH TO THE TEAM

TWO LEVELS OF SELF-SUFFICIENCY

If you organise affairs so that people are suitably self-sufficient it saves time and promotes goodwill. Having responsibility is motivational – people tend to do best those tasks for which they have personal responsibility.

There are two distinct levels of self-sufficiency in how people work:

- **Involvement.** This can be created in various ways such as: consultation, giving good information and making it clear that suggestions are welcome and that experiment and change in how things are done are good. **This provides the opportunity to contribute beyond the base job.**

- **Empowerment.** Empowerment adds the authority to be self-sufficient (making your own decisions) and creates the basis for people to become self-sufficient on an ongoing basis. **In a sense, empowerment creates a culture of involvement and gives it momentum.**

THE POWER OF RESPONSIBILITY

Together, involvement and empowerment create an environment in which people can have responsibility for their own actions. But remember:

*Responsibility cannot be given – it can only be taken; thus only the opportunity to **take** it can be given.*

Creating a situation in which people *do* take responsibility for their work demands:

- Clear objectives (people knowing exactly what they must do and why)
- Good communications
- Motivation (to show the desirability, for the individual as well as for the organisation, of taking responsibility)
- Trust (having created such a situation, you have to let people get on with things)

A team enjoying involvement in what they do, and having the authority to make decisions and get the job done, is the best recipe for successful management.

ADDING STRENGTH TO THE TEAM

A MANAGEMENT CATALYST

A successful team is one that:

- Is set up correctly
- Responds to the responsibility it has for the task
- Seeks constant improvement (and does not ever get stuck *on the tramlines*)
- Sees its manager as a fundamental support to its success

A team in this situation will do well and is more likely to go on doing well than a group just *told what to do*. **Your role is one of catalyst – constantly helping the team to keep up with events, to change in the light of events and to succeed because it is always configured for success.**

Working to maintain success

LOOKING AHEAD

> *My interest in
> the future is because I am going to
> spend the rest of my life there*
> Charles Kettering

All action that you take early
on must be predicated on the
necessity not only to create an
effective management relationship, but also to maintain it.
Thus, you need to consider alongside each other:

- **The short-term**. What will be the immediate impact of this? How will people
  respond? How will it affect the growing view people have of me as a manager? And
  will it *do the job*, get done whatever needs to be done, and get it done effectively?

- **The long-term**. Does this set an unfortunate precedent? Is this an approach that
  makes sense long-term? Even if this causes upset now, will the logic of it be clear
  later or will it be promptly forgotten?

**While matters of immediate urgency are, in a sense, a priority, always keep the
long-term in mind.**

MULTIPLE OBJECTIVES

Your job is to get things done – to achieve your objectives. Doing this demands that you win, and keep, the goodwill and support of your team. Therefore, get into the habit of considering:

- The effectiveness of your actions/decisions. Will they achieve the job that needs to be done?

- The way your actions/decisions will be perceived. How will other people react?

Sometimes the response is positive. People approve the decision and applaud you for the line you have taken. In this case you may want to maximise this effect. Sometimes you may feel that the response will be negative, in which case you may need to:

- Reconsider and select another way forward.

- Take the action, but explain why a particular approach is necessary.

- Compensate for the negative reaction. Perhaps you need to do something: you explain it but know it will still rankle, so you find an opportunity to balance it in some way, making it clear that it was exceptional.

NOTHING IS FOREVER

The environment in which you work is, no doubt, dynamic. Change is the order of the day. We may not know exactly what is coming but, during the course of your career as a manager, you can be sure that change will continue and that the pace of change will increase. Never forget this and help – and expect – your people to recognise it too.

As a manager you are effectively an agent for change. You must:

- Constantly review everything (including procedures, systems and policies) to anticipate what needs changing

- Involve your team in this process, both in identifying areas for change and in prompting ideas about how change should be made

- Always be open-minded, and create a culture of open-mindedness amongst your team

Challenging the status quo – asking *Why?* and actively prompting change – is a key part of your remit. Keep ahead; managing today using yesterday's methods will never keep your team with you.

MAINTAINING CREDIBILITY

If you act like a good manager, then people will believe you are a good manager. Many things already mentioned have influence here. In addition, bear in mind that:

- You are judged not by the number of times you fail, but by the number of your successes: keep an eye on the ratio

- You are more likely to succeed by sticking your neck out than by always playing it safe (though consideration and care are necessary)

- If you admit your mistakes, people will see that you are human and will help you avoid repeating them (and help themselves avoid making similar mistakes)

- You should never cut off your options until it is unavoidable; you may want the choice later

Now that you are a manager you have to operate in a way that creates a persona that inspires respect and confidence: **your success can rub off on others.**

BUILD ON SUCCESS

The ongoing success of you and your operation involves a cycle of activity:

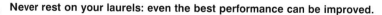

> **Understanding the**
> **key things that can create success**

> **Fine-tuning and building in the**
> **experience of how things worked to**
> **improve what you do next**

> **Being conscious of**
> **how you do things as you do them**

> **Monitoring the**
> **results arising from what you do**

> **Planning and**
> **acting in accordance with that**

 Never rest on your laurels: even the best performance can be improved.

SUMMARY
Key Issues

SUMMARY

KEEPING THE OVERALL MANAGEMENT PROCESS IN MIND

First, keep the key management functions in mind:

- Define objectives (your own and others)
- Plan (and time) action
- Communicate (throughout the process)
- Support others' action
- Evaluate performance (and link to the future)

Then relate this to the task, the team and the individual people.

WELL DONE!

KEEPING THE OVERALL MANAGEMENT PROCESS IN MIND

	Task	Team	Individual Needs
Define Objectives	Identify task and constraints	Set targets Involve team	Agree targets and responsibilities
Plan	Establish priorities Decide	Structure and delegate	Assess skills Train Delegate
Communicate	Brief and check understanding	Consult Obtain feedback	Listen Advise Enthuse
Support/Control	Monitor progress Check standards	Co-ordinate Reconcile conflict	Recognise Encourage Counsel
Evaluate	Review Re-plan Summarise	Reward success Learn from failure (and success)	Appraise, guide and train for the future

This view encapsulates, and simplifies, the whole process. With this picture in mind certain key issues are worth a mention as we summarise; see over.

LINK TO THE FUTURE

Before moving to key points in *Summary*, it is worth noting that we have come full circle. A good start is, of course, desirable in its own right. This is not just because it makes for a more comfortable transition for you, but because it brings better results. Thus ongoing success as a manager is influenced by:

- The attitude you take to the transition
- What you do before you move into a new appointment
- The *early* focus you bring to bear on key issues
- The relationship you thus cultivate with staff
- The working habits you create for yourself (and others) in the process

Together, all the above influence early success in the job – and how you take things forward into the future. **The opportunity of getting off to a good start may occur only once, but its effects are long-lived.**

SUMMARY

KEY ISSUES

From the beginning, always operate on the basis that managing people:

- **Takes time** – you cannot get so bound up in your own workload that you skimp on time you should spend with others

- **Takes effort** – it is a challenge, there are no magic formulae or quick fixes that will do the job for you

- **Needs thought** – the obvious or immediate answer may not be best, things may well need research, analysis and thinking through

- **Is not a solo effort** – seek and take advice from where you can, including your own staff

- **Will not always go right** – as Oscar Wilde said, *Experience is the name so many people give to their mistakes*; admit your mistakes (publicly if necessary) and learn from your experience

SUMMARY

KEY ISSUES

Remember too that managing people:

- **Is a process of helping others to be self-sufficient** – this implies trust and that management works best when you take a positive view of what people can do (and do not see your role as a sort of corporate *security guard*)

- **Is based on good, regular and open communication** – something that pervades many issues commented on in these pages

- **Needs to be acceptable to people before it can be effective** – hence the crucial role of motivation as part of the management task

- **Becomes self-sustaining when it works** – ie: if people find your management helpful (to the job, the organisation and to them) then they will support it and support you

Overall, management is not what you do to people but the process of how you work *with* people to help prompt their performance. Work *with* people from day one, and go on doing it throughout your management career.

KEY ISSUES

At the end of the day success comes down to a considered approach. Charge in, desperate to make an impression, go at everything at once in order to make an impression, and disaster may closely follow. And as was said at the beginning, first impressions last.

'Twas ever thus:

> *First organise the near at hand, then organise the far removed.*
> *First organise the inner, then organise the outer.*
> *First organise the basic, then organise the derivative.*
> *First organise the strong, then organise the weak.*
> *First organise the great, then organise the small.*
> *First organise yourself, then organise others.*
> Written by Chinese General Zhuge Liang nearly 2000 years ago

Perhaps we should highlight the last sentence: *First organise yourself, then organise others.*

LAST WORD

Being a manager is a challenge (this is where we started) but it is also almost infinitely rewarding to create and maintain a team of people who deliver excellent performance and produce whatever results are targeted.

As we have seen, it is a task that takes time, requires effort and needs a considered approach. Reading this book will not guarantee that you become CEO in the first six weeks (if you know what does that, let me know) but it may help you get firmly set on the initial rung of the ladder, and to go on from there.

Meantime, I suggest you always remember the old saying:

> *Never rely on good luck; it is only useful to explain why other people succeed*
> *(especially those you dislike!)*

So, I do not wish you luck but I wish you well with it. **All sorts of things can help, but only one person can guarantee that you become a good manager – and that's you.**

> *There are no short cuts to any place worth going*
> Beverly Sills

About the Author

Patrick Forsyth

Patrick runs Touchstone Training & Consultancy, an independent firm specialising in work in marketing, sales and management and communication skills. With more than twenty years' experience as a consultant, he has worked with clients in a wide range of industries and in many different parts of the world. He also conducts courses for a number of management institutes.

He is the author of five other Pocketbooks and a number of other successful business books including *Powerful Reports and Proposals*, *Marketing on a Tight Budget*, *Successful Time Management*, *Making Successful Presentations* and *Kickstart your Corporate Survival*. His books appear in more than ten languages; he also writes regularly for a number of business journals.

Contact

Patrick can be contacted at:
Touchstone Training & Consultancy, 28 Saltcote Maltings, Heybridge, Maldon, Essex CM9 4QP, U.K.
Tel/Fax: +44 (0)1621 859300   E-mail: patrick@touchstonetc.freeserve.co.uk

THE MANAGEMENT POCKETBOOK SERIES

Pocketbooks

Appraisals
Assertiveness
Balance Sheet
Business Planning
Business Writing
Call Centre Customer Care
Career Transition
Challengers
Coaching
Communicator's
Competencies
Controlling Absenteeism
Creative Manager's
C.R.M.
Cross-cultural Business
Cultural Gaffes
Customer Service
Decision-making
Developing People
Discipline
Diversity
E-commerce
Emotional Intelligence

Employment Law
Empowerment
Energy and Well-being
Facilitator's
Handling Complaints
Icebreakers
Impact & Presence
Improving Efficiency
Improving Profitability
Induction
Influencing
International Trade
Interviewer's
I.T. Trainer's
Key Account Manager's
Leadership
Learner's
Manager's
Managing Budgets
Managing Cashflow
Managing Change
Managing Upwards
Managing Your Appraisal

Marketing
Meetings
Mentoring
Motivation
Negotiator's
Networking
NLP
Openers & Closers
People Manager's
Performance Management
Personal Success
Positive Mental Attitude
Presentations
Problem Behaviour
Problem Solving
Project Management
Quality
Resolving Conflict
Sales Excellence
Salesperson's
Self-managed Development
Starting In Management
Stress .

Succeeding at Interviews
Teamworking
Telephone Skills
Telesales
Thinker's
Time Management
Trainer Standards
Trainer's
Training Evaluation
Training Needs Analysis
Vocal Skills

Pocketsquares

Great Training Robbery
Hook Your Audience

Pocketfiles

Trainer's Blue Pocketfile of
Ready-to-use Activities

Trainer's Green Pocketfile of
Ready-to-use Activities

Trainer's Red Pocketfile of
Ready-to-use Activities

ORDER FORM

Your details

Name _____

Position _____

Company _____

Address _____

_____

_____

Telephone _____

Facsimile _____

E-mail _____

VAT No. (EC companies) _____

Your Order Ref _____

Please send me:

		No. copies
The Starting in Management	Pocketbook	☐
The _____	Pocketbook	☐
The _____	Pocketbook	☐
The _____	Pocketbook	☐
The _____	Pocketbook	☐

Order by Post

MANAGEMENT POCKETBOOKS LTD
LAUREL HOUSE, STATION APPROACH, ALRESFORD,
HAMPSHIRE SO24 9JH UK

Order by Phone, Fax or Internet

Telephone: +44 (0)1962 735573
Facsimile: +44 (0)1962 733637
E-mail: sales@pocketbook.co.uk
Web: www.pocketbook.co.uk

Customers in USA should contact:
Stylus Publishing, LLC, 22883 Quicksilver Drive,
Sterling, VA 20166-2012
Telephone: 703 661 1581 or 800 232 0223
Facsimile: 703 661 1501 E-mail: styluspub@aol.com

Published by:
Management Pocketbooks Ltd
Laurel House, Station Approach, Alresford, Hants SO24 9JH, U.K.
Tel: +44 (0)1962 735573   Fax: +44 (0)1962 733637
E-mail: sales@pocketbook.co.uk
Website: www.pocketbook.co.uk

This edition published 2001.   Reprinted 2003, 2005.

© Patrick Forsyth 2001

ISBN 1 870471 87 3

British Library Cataloguing-in-Publication Data – A catalogue record for this book is available from the British Library.

Design, typesetting and graphics by **efex ltd.**   Printed in UK

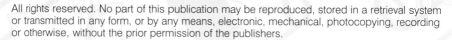